Yams

by Lada Josefa Kratky

NATIONAL GEOGRAPHIC
School Publishing

I am Yen. I am from here.
Do you see my big yam?

Have you had a yam? Yes or no? They are good. Oh yes, they are.

My job is to cut the yams.
I cut the bit with a bud.

I dig and dig. I put the
yam bit in the pit. The yam
can get wet. Mud is good for
a yam.

This bug is bad for a
yam. If I see this bug, I have
a job to do. If there are a
lot of bugs, this is a big job.

The yams get big. Can you see a yam yet? Yes, I can see a lot of yams.

Have a yam from Yen! Yum!